KIDS CAN WRITE!

KIDS CAN WRITE!

by

Lou Mathews

Louisa Mathews

Illustrated by Doug Grooms

A Hearthstone Book

Carlton Press, Inc.   New York, N.Y.

Dedicated to all the fourth, fifth, and sixth
grade kids who had to sit through my
classes in the Grover Hill Elementary
School. This is your book.

Out of respect to parents who may wish to preserve the privacy
of their families, the names of pupils, contributing to this book,
have been changed.

CONTENTS

INTRODUCTION

During a four-year period of my teaching career at Grover Hill Elementary school in Paulding County, Ohio, I became involved in a pilot project in creative writing. To tell the truth, at first I wasn't too anxious to participate. All sorts of questions went through my head: What if I couldn't think of enough activities to keep the kids interested? What if I couldn't get them interested right from the start? Several sleepless nights occurred while I fought with myself. Should I take part? Should I refuse?

I have always enjoyed writing stories and poems, especially for younger children. I like what I write: I do a terrific job? So-o-o, why can't I get involved with the students?

It finally dawned on me. "A-ha! Lou, you're afraid but not because the kids might not do as well as you expect. You're afraid of the reflection the results would have on you as the teacher if they did poorly."

I thought again, "I think my own stories are great and I like what I write. Why wouldn't the kids think the same about their work?"

After getting my head on straight and agreeing to take part in the project, we began to work. The students became more and more excited as each activity was completed. I think I became more excited than the students. They really amazed me: One activity, if it could be called an activity, was video taping our discussions before and after our writing. Being a "TV star" was a "shot in the arm" for every child in the class.

As a fourth grade teacher, it was much easier to have all the time we needed for activities for the project, since my class was self-contained. We took time whenever we needed it. It was more difficult when I transferred to fifth-sixth grades, which were departmentalized. I was allotted a forty-minute period each day for each class. It tied our hands, so to speak. There were times when we'd get to write only once or twice a month. Since we were rushed for time, we always had one or two discussions (not really enough) before we began to write. Even though we had very few chances to write, the results were great.

As you read these beautiful stories and poems, you will see that there are possibilities of good creative writing when correlated with any subject and it can be done by almost every child.

If you want them to write, give them a lot of encouragement and praise. Try it; they won't let you down:

PART I

Social Studies and Creative Writing

Social Studies can be rather boring to some students. Even I can't get too excited over learning dates, names, places, and events from years ago. Try working in some creative writing, which isn't boring at all. In fact, the kids will think they're getting "out of work" by doing it. They'll learn much from these pretend stories and poems. They won't realize they're learning because they'll be having fun using their imagination. Don't let them know they're learning; that would be like sticking a pin into a balloon:

The Pirate, Blackbeard

Blackbeard, the pirate, was as rough as could be
Sailed the oceans in 1393.
He wore a large hat and carried a sword
and frightened the passengers when they came aboard.
He took their jewels, their money, their gold.
If they refused—"Walk the plank:" they were told.
Many cried, "The ship we must save:"
But Blackbeard put them into a watery grave:

John Soder

The Pirates

Pirates, pirates,
of the Spanish Main.
They had been traveling
and soon hit Spain.

They had big mouths
to carry their knives.
Some people they did kill
and others, they spared their lives.

Norman Lockridge

9

The Pirates

There are fat pirates and skinny pirates
but all of them are mean pirates
Blackbeard is the worst.
He has hair from head to toe.
Captain Hook is another bad one.
He is mean and has a hook for a hand.
Now—if Hook and Blackbeard should meet,
I wonder what would happen.

Colby Shaw

Pirates

The pirate ships roam the sea,
While others are lost in some hidden bay,
Some pirates drink rum, others drink tea,
That's their reason for being happy and gay.

They steal all the gold
All valuable pieces of coin,
They save some of their loot
But, like most everyone else
They spend it everytime they land.

Samuel Weiner

Pirate Blackbeard

Pirate Blackbeard
by everyone is feared.
I would never laugh at him
He would just raise his gun.

He, one day, met his match
He didn't get just a scratch
He got a bullet through his chest
At the bottom of the ocean, he lies at rest.

David Entratta

10

The Spanish Main, Home of the Pirates

Brave men sailed with their treasure ships
Heading for countries both near and faraway
But not for long, when the pirates struck
And took their treasures, to them, big pay.

They killed brave men and searched their ships
The ships were then sunk and buried below
In the warm blue waters on the ocean floor
Their secrets were hidden, never to be known.

Terry Shilson

The Great Great Day

One day I went to the great fair at Montreal. I wanted to look around so I walked to the middle of the fair. I saw men shooting guns. I also heard the governor welcome the Indians to the fair. I saw a man and an Indian trading things.

Later, I played some games, ran races, and BOY, was that fun: I also watched a shooting contest between boys my age. That night, we sang and danced by the campfire. I danced with a sailor who was a little smaller than I but we still had lots of fun.

It was soon time to go home. I thought about the wonderful day I had had at the fair. I said to my dad, "That was a really great, great day:"

Elizabeth Dawes

The Big Day

You don't know this but I get to go to that big fair at Montreal. I am one of the "things" for sale. I'm a pair of fur lined boots.

It seems as if everyone is here. I can see everything from where I am standing. The boys and girls are having fun. The men are smoking peace pipes, one right after another. People come every day to the fair without getting tired of it. They all play games. There are boats in the water. Everything you need is here. There is everything from furs to guns.

At the end of the day everyone is tired and begin their long journey home. But early tomorrow morning they will be back.

11

I hope some nice boy or girl will buy me and take me home with them. I will keep their feet warm for a long long time.

Micki Schultz

No Carnival for Maria

Poor Maria couldn't go to the carnival.
She wanted so badly to go the carnival.
She wished and wished but no boy would come.

The carnival would be there everyday,
All the people who lived in Brazil
would be there—all but Maria.
She felt sad to be the only girl
who wouldn't be at the carnival.

Louise Becker

The Carnival

The carnival is here.
It's the "funnest" time of the year.
We girls are dancing
while the horses are prancing.

The clowns are performing
while everyone is visiting.
The carnival will soon be over.
We will have to wait 'till next October
for another carnival.

Mary Anson

What a Day!!

I am an Indian boy. I am at a great fair here in Montreal. There are a lot of people here and lots of things to see, do, and buy. There are more Indians than there are Frenchmen because the Indians want more furs for the winter.

We play games, run races, and engage in shooting contests. I will make a lot of friends and learn many good games from the white boys and girls.

People are here from Quebec, Gape, Newfoundland, Nova Scotia, and the Gulf of the St. Lawrence River. The Algonquin Indians are here, too. There are also farmers here to trade their farm products.

Guess who I shook hands with this morning—Cartier, Champlain, LaSalle, and many other French explorers. It was a very good day.

Tim

Indians Trade

"Now we have to wrap up the furs," said Brave Bear, "so they will be ready for the big trade fair tomorrow. If we sell all the furs, I might get you a knife, Little Eagle."

I would like that," answered Little Eagle with a big grin. "Then I can go kill Big Black Bear."

"You are too little to go hunting alone, Little Eagle," replied Brave Bear.

The next day Brave Bear and Little Eagle took the furs to the fair. Brave Bear traded some of the furs for sacks of corn. He also traded for his gun. He looked at the knives. He knew he must have one for his son, Little Eagle.

Little Eagle came up to his father and asked, "Did you get me a knife, father?"

Brave Bear answered and patted Little Eagle on the head, "Yes, my son, here is your knife."

Little Eagle took his knife and thanked his father for it. The furs were given to the trader as pay for the knife. Little Eagle and his father then went home.

Two years later, Little Eagle killed Big Black Bear with the knife his father had given him. Brave Bear was very proud of his son. Little Eagle was now one of the bravest warriors of the tribe.

Rick

A Day at the Fair

I am an Indian boy. My name is Little Eagle. My father and I are going to the fair. Father has an armful of furs.

When we arrived at the fair, Father began trading his furs. He traded for knives, cloth, and pots and pans.

It was fun playing with the boys who had come on the ships. I taught one boy how to shoot a bow and arrow so he taught me to shoot a gun.

I know I will go to the fair again next year. I don't think I will ever miss a single fair at Montreal.

Cliff

14

What a Day!

The town was very happy because tomorrow the Yankee Peddler arrives. I thought I was the happiest girl in town. All I could think of was what I wanted to buy from the Yankee Peddler. He didn't come very often.

It was really hard to sleep that night because all I could think of was the Yankee Peddler.

Next morning came suddenly. I thought of what I wanted so very much. It was a new pair of shoes.

Finally the Yankee Peddler arrived. I was so excited: All I could think of was a new pair of shoes. He had a lot of customers so I had to wait a long time before it was my turn.

He came up to me, at last, and asked, "What would you like, young lady?"

I told him I wanted a pair of shoes. He had the right size for me. Oh, I was so happy that he had had just what I wanted:

This has been the happiest day of my life. I can hardly wait 'till the Yankee Peddler comes next year.

Carol

The Yankee Peddler

The Yankee Peddler came one day. He had knives, food, candy, furniture, cloth, and many other items. I bought a knife. My sister got a doll and a book. We both got some candy. Mom got some pots, pans, cloth, and some vegetables.

When we had everything we wanted, we invited the Yankee Peddler into the house for supper. He always stopped at our house after that because he knew that he would always be invited to eat supper with us and have some of Mom's good applie pie.

Dean

The Yankee Peddler

When I was a boy, it was a great day when the Yankee Peddler came. I bought many things and he always stayed over-night to tell us what had happened since the last time he had been there.

He told us that the engineers had finished the Erie Canal. So we decided to pack up and head west. We started from New York and sailed up the Hudson River to Albany. When we were in Albany we stopped at an inn. We got up early the next morning and started the long trip to Buffalo. We went by meadows and pastures. We saw many things that were new to us. When we arrived at Buffalo, my father decided to buy some land about ten miles outside Buffalo.

My family and I worked very hard to build a house and barn. We finally finished them. We had settled in a nice peaceful place.

Greg G.

Our Home in the West

We finally stopped and settled down. It was about seven at night. Everyone was really tired so we all went to bed.

In the morning, I had to walk to the stream and get a bucket of water. My dad, my brothers, and I began clearing the land. We used some of the big trees for the cabin. When we rested, we either lay in the wagon or sat under the trees.

The next week we started to build the barn since we had finished the house late Saturday night. We were just finishing the barn when I hit my thumb trying to nail a board above one of the windows.

It took almost a month to build a barn. Our next project was a fence. It didn't take very long to do that since we really didn't do a very good job.

Next year we will do some farming and help some of the new settlers get settled.

Rick

My Life as a Slave

My name is Louise Jefferson. I live with my father, mother, and little brother in our slave cabin. We live near a city called Norfolk, Virginia. It is located near the Atlantic Ocean so our master's farm products can be loaded and shipped easily to other parts of the world.

We work for the Smith family. My father, brother, and I work on the plantation. We are called field hands. We plant and care for the cotton fields. When the cotton is ready, we pick it and have it ready to be loaded and sent away. We get up at sunrise and work hard until the sun sets. We hardly ever have meat to eat unless our master gives us some for a special occasion.

We live in a log cabin. In the wintertime our cabin is very cold. The snow blows in the cracks. We sleep on bundles of straw on the dirt floor. I sure wish I could sleep on a soft bed some night. We are lucky enough to have a plank table to eat from and wooden benches to sit on. We eat our food from wooden bowls. We have a garden plot in back of the cabin where we raise our own food.

One hot summer day my brother and I were out in the cotton field. We saw a boy being beaten for not working. At that moment we decided to run for our freedom. While no one was watching us, we ran as fast as we could. The bloodhounds tracked us down later that day. When they found us, we were beaten and dragged back to the plantation. From then on, our owners watched more closely. I hope slavery is abolished and my family and I can be free to live as we wish.

Laura

I Was a Slave

I was born in Charleston, West Virginia, on a plantation owned by William Garver. I work in a field, hoeing weeds or plowing for my master all day long.

My grandfather is a butler in the house. My mother is one of the cooks. I have two brothers who live in Richmond. They work on the docks, loading tobacco and cotton. My father is dead. He tried to escape from slavery in 1875. He was found twenty miles away and was shot.

I was sold when I was thirteen years old. William Garver bought me, my grandfather, and my mother for three-hundred dollars.

I remember trying to run away when I was sixteen. I was about three miles away before the bloodhounds tracked me down. I was taken back and beaten with a whip. That is all they did to me. It was enough. But sometimes they put runaways in cages for three days. Or they might take an axe and cut off the runaway's toes. Then they can't run away again.

I was taught to read and write when I was twenty years old by a seventeen-year-old slave named Amos, whom Mr. Garver had bought in Huntington. Amos had been taught by his previous owner's children.

Mark

PART II

Spelling and Creative Writing

I can hear you saying, "What a dumb title—spelling and Creative Writing...." Before you get too hysterical, read on:

How about choosing one word from the week's spelling list and using it as a title for a story or a poem? This is fun, fun, fun! As you will read, they really liked writing about the teacher. I told them anything would be okay as long as they didn't get insulting. I didn't "come out" too badly, did I? Most of the kids enjoyed using "people" words, especially members of their families. They also wanted to write about the country and the "city," depending on where they lived. (Ours is a rural community, with several small villages scattered about within the school district.)

Children

Some are fat and some are thin,
Some are funny and some are not.
Some have green eyes and some have blue,
Some have red hair and some have brown.
Some are tall and some are small.
Some are girls and some are boys.
Some like to work and some do not.
Some are eight and some are nine.
Some get 100s and some do not.
Some like summer and some like fall.
Some like spelling and some do not.
Some like orange and some like red.
Some like teachers and some do not.
But on the average, children are great people!

May Aarons

Children

Some children are fat and some are skinny.
Some are good and some are bad.
Some are big and some are little.
Some eat a lot and some don't.
Some have long hair and some have short hair.
Some are boys and some are girls.

Sydanna Brown

My Teacher

My teacher is fun. She lets us talk sometimes. She lets us march in the mornings. Do you know where she gets all her "go?" She gets it from all us kids. But then, after lunch, we do math. That's hard on us. We want to play. She is just too young to understand.

Luke

My Teacher

My teacher has red hair and a temper to go with it. She now has a ten-ton cast on her leg and that doesn't help matters. She

19

writes stories and poems. She sometimes writes stories about us. But I guess she's okay.

Jane Terry

My Teacher

My teacher's name is Mrs. Mathews and she is the nicest teacher I know. Even if she has a bad leg and needs us kids to help her get around. She can still paddle hard. About as hard as the principal. She is still the nicest teacher.

My Teacher

At times she gets very mad at us, be we don't care. She is real nice and a friend most of the time. But when it's your birthday, watch out! If you're a boy you get a kiss from her. But if you're a girl, it's worse! You get about ten cracks with the paddle. We really like her. She is lots of fun.

Wendy

My Teacher

My teacher's name is Mrs. Mathews. I like her and I wish I could stay in the fourth grade forever. She is always joking around. The best thing about her is that she never gives very much homework. She has pretty red hair and has a great personality. She is a great teacher and a good friend.

Harold

PART III
The Business Letter and Creative Writing

"Class, for tomorrow's assignment rewrite the business letter on page 133. Be sure to place each part of the letter in the correct place." That's terrible! Have you ever read fifty identical business letters from a group of fifth graders? Ugh! Pure torture for the kids but more so for the teacher! How about using the exercises in the book for discussion, for writing on the board, *practice* for seat work, etc.? Then, try creative writing for the "real thing."

We did just this, and the kids did a perfect job—almost. They chose their "companies" and everything that goes with a business letter. After you have read the following "business letters," I think you'll agree that they are far more interesting than any letter you'll read in a texbook.

Dora's Diaper Service
148 Baby Lane
Babyland Ohio 46589

R.R. 4
Grover Hill, Ohio 45849
December 14, 1981

Dear Ladies:

I would like to order some more of your Wonder Diapers. My baby really loves them. Please send me two-hundred boxes because of the long hard winter ahead.

Sincerely,
Taylor Kane

Mrs. Janie Malary
Six Will Drive
Six Fingers, Florida 34562

Box 22
Scott, Ohio 45886
December 14, 1981

Mrs. Mallary:

Please send me a pair of your best winter gloves. Make sure the left glove has six fingers. I happen to have six fingers and a thumb on my left hand. Enclosed is a check for two dollars and fifty cents.

Sincerely,
Joe T.

Tom Scratch
Itchie Street
Dogcollar, Ohio 57923

Rt. 1
Paulding, Ohio 45879
December 14, 1981

Dear Mr. Scratch:

I understand you have the biggest flea factory in the world. Please send me one of your best fleas. My dog needs a friend.

Sincerely,
Billy V.

Roger Lens
18 Eyeball Rd.
Glasses, Ohio 21212

Rt. 1, Box 31
Haviland, Ohio 45851
December 14, 1981

Dear Mr. Lens:
   Please send me a pair of your eyeglasses with three lenses. I happen to have three eyes and need that kind. Thank you.
                                        Sincerely,
                                        Tom Jack

Special Umbrella Co.
Stormy Valley
Rainsville, Ohio 24689

Rt. 1, Box 27A
Haviland, Ohio 45851
December 15, 1981

Dear Sir:
   Please, oh, please, send me an umbrella right away! My friends tell me it is going to rain cats and dogs on Thursday. Thank you and hurry!
                                        Sincerely,
                                        Kim Yun

PART IV

Seasons and Holidays

No doubt, this is when most teachers do creative writing. I see nothing wrong with using the seasons and holidays but I think there're many more opportunities to be had other than just seasons and holidays. I'm afraid that at times, these two topics are "run in the ground."

Not too many students will write seriously, especially about the true meaning of Easter and Christmas. Their stories and poems are usually full of fun and expectations.

The Lost Easter Egg

The Easter Bunny was hiding his eggs. He was at the last house but he had forgotten he had put one egg into his pocket because it wouldn't fit into the basket.

"Oh my, I've lost little Susie's egg! I must retrace my steps and find it!"

He had to travel all over the world. He looked in shoes. He looked in hats, coats, in fish bowls, in the flowers—even under the chairs in the kitchen. He looked in the food, in Mother's purse, in the doghouse—everywhere! He was already to give up so he lay down to rest. Something was in his pocket. He slowly put in his hand. He pulled it out, just as slowly. There was his lost egg!

He hurried to Susie's house. He put the egg into her Easter basket. Just in time, too. Susie was coming down the stairs.

"Boy," said the Easter Bunny to himself, as he hurried away. "That was too close for comfort. I'll be more careful next time."

And he has always been more careful since then!

Lou

Easter Town

One day, in Easter Town, there was a big fight because Hank didn't believe in the Easter Bunny. Hank fought with Terry who did believe in the Easter Bunny.

Then someone said, "Why don't you two boys wait for the

Easter Bunny tonight?"

They agreed to wait together. They waited and waited and waited. They became very sleepy and both boys soon fell asleep.

While they were sleeping, the Easter Bunny came and hid the eggs. When they woke up, they hunted for the eggs and found every single one of them.

Later, that night, Hank turned to Terry and said, "You were right, Terry. There really is an Easter Bunny. And next year, if anyone says there isn't an Easter Bunny, I'll just have to fight him."

This was the best Easter that Easter Town ever had. You can just ask Hank and Terry.

Chris

The Lost Easter Egg

It was Easter morning when they had an Easter egg hunt. There were thirty eggs in all and I was one of them. The mother and father had hidden all of us. They put me up on the highest branch of the tree standing in their backyard.

They called the children to come and find the eggs. They found all of us except me.

The next morning the wind began to blow and I fell out of the tree. I broke into a million pieces when I hit the sidewalk. One of the boys came along and saw me. He saw that I was broken. He picked me up and glued me back together.

I am one lucky egg. I wasn't lost anymore and I lived in his bedroom until the day I died.

John

Easter

Easter is when the bunny comes hopping down the lane so green. Easter is all around us; just look and see. Look at all the signs of Easter. All the children are being good so the Easter Bunny will come to their houses. Easter is on its way now. See it coming, driving in its car.

Barbie

He Has Risen

I was guarding the tomb where Jesus was buried. It was three days after they had killed Him. Mary and her friends were coming to the tomb to put spices on Jesus's body.

I had fallen asleep. I knew no one could have moved the stone but when I awoke, the stone had been moved and Jesus was gone.

An angel spoke to Mary and her friends, "Jesus is not here. He has risen from the dead."

Mary went to tell the disciples, "Jesus has risen from the dead!"

She brought them back to the tomb. They saw the same thing. Jesus wasn't there. He had truly risen on the third day, just as He said He would!

We celebrate Easter for this reason. Jesus kept His promise. He died for you and me and arose from the dead on the third day.

Sean

The Sorrowful Day

One day one of the king's guards came and told me that I would have to nail Jesus to the cross. I'd have to whip Him, put thorns on His head, and spit in His face. I couldn't imagine such a terrible thing happening! I begged the king to get another man to do it but the king said I was the one he had chosen and I had to do it or be killed.

The time came. I went out to dig the hole in which the cross would be dropped. I felt like running away but I knew if I tried to run, the king would have me killed.

They made Jesus carry His own cross down the street. He had many wounds. I could see the rubbing of the cross on His shoulder. I could see how much Jesus was suffering. We came to the hole where the cross was to be dropped. They stripped Jesus of His garments and all the wounds opened. They stretched His arms across the wooden cross and I nailed Him to the cross.

When we dropped the cross that held Jesus, I knew He felt great pain in His hands and feet where I had put the nails. There He died.

We buried Him. But on the third day, He rose from the dead. I hope that I never have to do such a thing again, not to anyone, as I had to do to Jesus.

Why We Have Easter

A long time ago, in Bible times, Jesus was going to be crucified to save you and me from our sins. On the day before He was going to die, He prayed for a long time. Jesus didn't want to die but He wanted to obey God.

The soldiers who had taken Him to the cross didn't want Him to die either but they had to obey the king or they would be killed. They even made Jesus carry His own cross to the hill.

They nailed Him to the cross between two bad men. They made a thorn crown for Him and pushed it onto His head. He was thirsty and they gave Him vinegar to drink. They put a sword into His side to make sure He would die. He soon died and they placed Him in a tomb and rolled a big stone over the entrance so no one would try to take His body. They even had guards to watch so no one would bother the tomb.

Early Sunday morning, two women came to the tomb. The stone had been rolled away; the tomb was empty. Jesus was gone!

Jesus was gone but an angel came and told the women, "Don't be afraid."

The women cried, "Jesus had been stolen!" They sat outside the tomb and cried. Suddenly a voice spoke to them, "What is the matter?"

They answered, "Jesus's body has been stolen!"

Then they looked up to see who had spoken to them. It was Jesus!

The women were so happy that they ran to tell everyone. "He is not dead! He has risen from the dead as He told us He would!"

This is why we celebrate Easter. Jesus kept His promise.

Linda

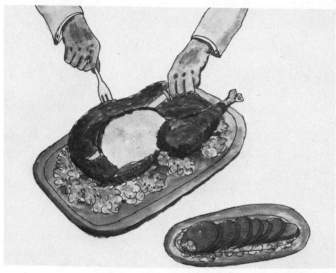

Thanksgiving Is...

something good to eat
no school.
relatives come over.
thanking God for our food.
thankful for what peace we have in our country.
good smells in the house.
thanking God for everything.

Maria

What Thanksgiving Is to Me

I thank God for Thanksgiving because He helped the Pilgrims across the angry waves of the ocean to come to America and have their feast that made our first Thanksgiving. Even though some got sick and some died, some also made it to America.

Laurie

Thanksgiving

Hello, my name is Brenda. I want to tell you what Thanksgiving means to me. I like Thanksgiving because we get to have a great feast. We eat all day. Another reason is that we get out of school. I like it because it reminds me when my brother was married last Thanksgiving.

Brenda

What Christmas Means to Me

Christmas means different things to different people. To me, Christmas means that I will see all of my family together. I will watch my mom bake cookies and cakes. I will receive gifts, but best of all, give something to many other people.

Christmas also means it was the date long ago that God sent His only son, Jesus, to help all mankind. This is what Christmas means to me.

Chiang

Christmas

Christmas means a lot to me. Christmas is when you get gifts, give parties, and have family get-togethers. It means Christmas plays at church. But most of all, it means when Christ was born so many years ago. It was when Mary and Joseph went to Bethlehem. They asked the innkeeper for a room. He said he didn't have any rooms but there was room in the stable.

Jesus's birthday has always been on December 25th and we have had Christmas on that day ever since.

Joseph

What Christmas Means to Me

   Christmas is the time for laughter, fun, and play. We give gifts to our relatives and best friends. It is time to decorate the tree and put lights outside to make other people happy. It is the time to remember Christ. Christ was born on Christmas Eve. Later, he gave His life for us.

Ed

Christmas Means...

putting bulbs on the tree.
opening presents.
riding around and looking at decorated houses.
putting bulbs outside.
going to church and practicing the Christmas play.
But thinking about Jesus is really the most important thing.

Morris

Christmas Is Fun

Christmas means a tree and decorations. It also means Mother is busy shopping and getting home late.

We are always ready for Christmas morning. There are gifts for everyone. It is nice to be together and to be happy. But best of all, we get out of school for a week or two!

What Christmas Means to Me

Most of all, we celebrate the day Jesus was born. Christmas means that I will have someone to play with. This year everyone in the family is coming to our house. All of the kids will be playing in the garage. Not the real little ones. We will get to unwrap presents and then get to play with the toys we receive. That is what Christmas means to me.

Warren

What Christmas Means to Me.

Christmas means to me that Jesus was born in the manger with a bright star over the manger, with Mary and Joseph and the shepherds and wisemen who saw the star from afar.

Early

A Very Scary Night

One cold and windy night I lost my way in the forest. I saw a light. It was a light in a robbers' den. They took me in. I was really scared. I jumped out the window and ran home. I told my dad what had happened. The next morning my dad went to the den. It had been some school kids having a Halloween party.

Tom S.

The Scared Goblin

One Halloween night there was a goblin who was afraid of his own shadow. One night he tried to scare some boys but when he saw his shadow he ran back to his house. The mother goblin told him it was just his shadow. He was never afraid of it again.

Tom W.

Halloween

Halloween is when the black cats walk in front of you. The owls enjoy themselves. The bats bite. They even knock on doors. That's what Halloween is to me!

Tom K.

Halloween

Halloween is the time when you go trick or treating and wear spooky masks. Then you get sick from all the candy you eat. Your mom tells you that you shouldn't have eaten so much of your candy.

Max

Halloween

Halloween is the time for mothers to get the Pepto-Bismal ready. It is the time for kids to dress up in ghost and goblin outfits. Halloween is the time for you to soap windows. It is when you put your pumpkin faces on your front porch. It's the time to visit the graveyard, to rattle chains, and to scare people. It is the time to go trick or treating. It's the time to see hundreds of witches on their broomsticks riding in the sky. Halloween is a fun time.

Mandy

The Screech

It was a scary Halloween night. All of a sudden there was a screech. It sounded like this, "E-e-e-e-k!" I wondered what it was. I heard it again and again. I was really scared. I got my flashlight and looked for it. I found a mouse in one of my mom's mousetraps.

Howard

Boo!!!

Last night I heard something. It sounded like "BOO." I went outside to see what it was. It was so dark that I couldn't see anything so I went back into the house and got my flashlight and then came back out again. I saw a goose talking to my dog. I went up to the goose but it wouldn't talk to me. I turned around and there stood a ghost. I was really scared! All at once the ghost started to laugh. It was my brother.

Mara

The Storm

We had a storm last night.
I was really really scared.
My mother screamed.
My brother laughed.
My father jumped
and shook the whole house.
I was the only one really scared.

Keri

A Storm

A storm is wind blowing.
A storm is grass blowing.
A storm is trees blowing.
A storm is thunder and lightning.

Mitch

PART V

Similes, Metaphors, and Personifications

Similes, metaphors, and personification—you'll never "meet" these three on the street! They have to be "invented" by good writers. Read the following stories and you will almost feel as if you had taken the walks with us. (Come to think of it, maybe I was wrong. Maybe we did "meet" these three on the street!)

Our Walk Through Town

As we left our school to begin our walk, we could smell smoke which smelled like my father's barbecuing. As we walked past some trees, we thought the leaves and branches looked like my mother right after she washed her hair. The smell from the lilac bushes reminded me of my sister right after she took a bath.

We walked down the road. The tar was sticky and it felt like we were walking through triple-rubber-bubble gum.

We went to the Dairy Queen and our great teacher treated us to ice cream cones.

We went back to the playground and played games. We ran as gracefully as pigs in ballet suits.

Bonnie

Things We Saw As We Walked

The cars were going by looking as if they were puffing cigars. The tractors were yelling at the mill because the wagons were hard to pull. The wind was pushing the grass to make it dance.

Sherman

Our Trip

On our trip, I heard a bird that sounded like it was playing a flute. The grass smelled like fresh cut hay. I could feel the stones under my feet and I felt as if I was walking on beans.

When we came back to our classroom, we sang songs. We sounded like hound dogs that had treed a coon. We played follow-the-leader as if we didn't have one.

Mike

Imagination Is Funny

I took a walk one day. The leaves were changing color. I thought I could hear them saying, "How do you like our new dresses?" I could hear the birds. I saw that one was very angry with another. She was telling him that he was very lazy. I saw leaves on the ground. They were dead. The wind was blowing them, as if she was trying to wake them. I heard a hammer. It sounded like thunder. Isn't your imagination funny?

Donna

My Adventure

When I was walking, I heard a radio. It sounded like my mom and sister gossiping. When I saw my ice cream cone, it reminded me of a snow covered mountain. When I tasted my ice cream, it tasted like a Big Chef, french fries, and root beer—all at one time. When I felt the tar on the road, I thought I was walking through quicksand. When I passed one house where a man was mowing the grass, it smelled almost as good as a hamburger.

Louis

A Trip Through Imagination

When we went on our walk I could hear our footsteps. They sounded like a mixed up army marching. I could feel my ice cream on my lips. It made me feel as if I was in a snowball. I could taste my ice cream. It tasted as good as my mom's apple pie. I could see tulips in a flower garden. They looked like a brand new rainbow. When we sang we sounded as bad as a mixed up choir.

Hubert

PART VI
Wishing—
A Special Place of My Own

Kids are always wishing. They usually know exactly what they want. They hardly ever wish for just one thing. Even though I'm not much of a kid, I love to wish, too!

Most everyone, not just kids, have, or would like to have, a secret place to call their own where they can go and not be bothered, where they can pretend to the fullest, where their "pretending" can become "real" because it's their secret place. There's no one around to laugh or to tell them to grow up. If you are lucky enough to have such a place, don't tell anyone where it is!

'If I Were a Magician, I Would...

bake a cake in my hat.
disappear after supper so I wouldn't have to do the dishes.
turn my brother into a frog and throw him out the back door.

37

make my eight puppies old enough to hold.
turn my boyfriend into a prince.

A.R.

If I Was a Magician

If I was a magician I would work in a great circus. I would turn dogs into cats and cats into dogs. I would make things disappear and make handkerchiefs float through the air.

D.D.

If I Was a Magician

I would make dreams come true.
I would wish for $1,000.
I would do a lot of tricks for people.
I would make grade cards disappear forever.

R.D.

If I Was a Magician

I would send my brother to the moon.
I would do tricks in front of hundreds of people for lots of money.
I would have the report cards and paddles disappear from every teacher's desk.

L.R.

Wishing, Wishing, Wishing

If I was to wish for somethin' to eat
I'd wish for a great big treat.
It would be somethin' sweet.

It isn't good for you
and it isn't good for me—
I like to eat candy.

A.L.

My Impossible Dream

I have an impossible dream of my own and I will tell you about it. I wish I could be millions of things, like a star football player. I dream of being a baseball player and have sixty-one home runs in one year. I would like to be the President of the United States and rule our country. But then, sometimes, I just like to be myself, just like I am.

M.R.

A Mad Mother

One night, I had a dream. I have always wanted a fire truck and, in my dream, my bed had turned into one. My bedposts were ladders, the headboard was the steering wheel, and my pillow was the water hose. The alarm clock rang. I shouted, "Fire! Fire!"

The fire was at the Miller house. It was almost burned down when I got there. I began spraying water on the fire. I thought to myself, "This water doesn't look like water."

I woke up and saw that I was "spraying" pillow feathers. Boy, was my mom ever mad when she came into my room and saw what I had done to the pillow!

B.M.

PART VII
"Saying Good-bye to an Old Friend"

The new school building was "growing" while we still "worked" in the old. We talked about how the old school might be feeling as it watched the new school becoming more beautiful as the days passed, and knowing, because it was old, it was soon to be destroyed and replaced by the new school.

The Old and the New

Looking around me, I see the new Grover Hill School becoming more complete every day. Everything about it looks so shiny and new.

Here I am, the old Grover Hill School, standing where I have stood for seventy-one years. My plumbing is bad. The janitor is constantly working on it. In the new building they will have all new and modern plumbing.

My blackboards are chipped and it gets harder to write on them everday. My furnace doesn't work very well. Sometimes it gets so cold that the children have to wear their coats.

My walls are cracked and have shoe prints all over them. Some of the walls have been repainted but they still don't look that great.

I will be torn down soon. I hope the new building will last as long as I have and that seventy-one years from now, children will still be attending school here at Grover Hill.

A.G.

I Am Old

Hi! I am the Grover Hill School in Grover Hill. I am going to be replaced by a young new school beside me. It's all because my roofs are leaking, some of my windows are broken, and my heaters aren't working half the time.

I was built in 1911 and I have gotten pretty bad as the years passed by. When I first came along, I knew that some day I would be replaced by a new school. Sitting in one place for seventy-one years makes even a school house kind of tired.

Over the years, many thousands of students have been taught in my classrooms. When I get demolished, I will always remember things and events that have happened in my classrooms and in my gymnasium.

C.K.

I was constructed in 1911 and am three stories tall. I was nice and young then but now I'm getting old. My floors are all creaky and bent. The kids are always stomping on me and wiping mud on me.

My walls are cracked and my paint is peeling. My rooms are all dusty and run down. My radiators don't work half the time and then I get cold along with the children. My ceiling leaks and my moldings are falling.

My teachers are getting old, too, but that doesn't matter. I'm going to miss the kids and the teachers. The new building thinks that it knows everything. It has new carpet and fancy windows. I'm going to miss everything and everyone when I'm gone.

V.C.

I was born in 1911 and that makes me seventy-one years old. I'm going to retire in the summer of '83. I will tell you why.

My ceilings are falling apart because when it rains the roof leaks and this has loosened my plaster. My floors are "oil-logged" because they have been oiled alot. There are even holes in the floors. The wooden floors are "dug up" where some of the seats have been scooted back and forth. My walls are full of cracks. There are streaks on them where the water has leaked in and run down the walls when it rained real hard. My heaters work sometimes and sometimes they don't. It's either too hot or too cold, hardly ever just right.

Y.B.

PART VIII
Tall and Taller Tales

The sixth grade students have been studying and writing tall tales. Roy Rider of Cleveland, Ohio, a writer of tall tales, permitted the class to use his story, "The Roasted Snowflakes," as part of the lesson. After the students had read Mr. Rider's story, we discussed it with much excitement and then they wrote their own tall tales. Mr. Rider also visited and spoke to the students. When Mr. Rider saw the corporation sign of Van Wert and noticed the similarity between Van Wert and Van Winkle, he suggested to the students about writing stories entitled "Rip Van Wert." After reading the story of "Rip Van Winkle," the class came up with their own stories of "Rip Van Wert."

Rip Van Wert

Once upon a time there lived a man named Rip Van Wert. He was an old-timer who was born in the year 1352. He had a foot-long beard. His wife's name was Dame Van Wert. They lived with their two children, Scott and Seth.

They had a thirty-acre farm. They had thirty-three horses, fifty-seven chickens, and thirty-six pigs.

One day Rip was coming home from the Red Wert Inn. When he got home, he went into the barn to put the horses away. Dame and the boys were doing the chores.

As soon as his wife saw him she screamed, "Why, you ol' lazy good-for-nothin' thing! You go everywhere but you will never stay at home and work on your farm!" She grabbed a broom from nearby and kept whacking him with it. She finally convinced Rip he should help her and the boys with the work.

One day Rip was plowing his thirty-acre field when something made him look up. He saw something weird in the sky, something like a spaceship. He unhitched the plow, climbed onto the horse and rode to the house. He got his gun and rode to where the spaceship had landed.

When we got there he hid in the bushes. Just when he thought he we well hidden, something grabbed him by the shoulder. Rip turned around and saw this green thing. It was shaped like a cow.

They took him and went into the spaceship. The green thing

42

handed a bottle to Rip and said, "Drink this."

Rip asked, "What is it?"

"It's beer!"

"Beer?"

"Yeah, beer. Go on and drink it."

So Rip drank it and he really liked it!

Later on, after many beers, the spaceship landed and Rip climbed out. He climbed onto his horse and rode back home to tell his wife and boys of his adventure. They all listened. When he finished his story, his wife sneered and said, "When and where in tarnation did you see something like that?"

Rip answered, "I saw that thing and the spaceship when I was plowing. I really did."

The next day he went into town and told the town's people his story. That's how beer was discovered.

C.S.

Tallest Tale Ever

On July eight, my tenth birthday, I received a baby chicken from my Uncle Fred. He's a farmer who lives in Missouri. Uncle Fred taught me a few things I needed to know about raising a chick. He even helped me name it. We decided to name him Frederick since it was Uncle Fred who had given me the gift.

As years passed, Frederick grew bigger and bigger. For my twelfth birthday, I was given a special pen for him. He wasn't a baby chick anymore. He was full grown. In fact, he was over-grown. He was now twelve feet tall and weighed four-hundred-fifty pounds!

Everyday all the kids in George Town would come over to ride Frederick. He would take four or five kids for a ride at the same time, so everyone would get a chance to ride.

Frederick and I had some good times. He even played catch with me. 'til one day the chicken catcher came and took him away. I really don't feel sad 'cause Frederick is now in show business, making more money than Bo Derek.

T.T.

The Surprise Egg

One day I went to the store to buy a carton of eggs. When I got home and opened the carton, there was one big brown egg in the carton. I cracked the brown egg and out came a miniature horse with wings. I ran to tell my mom what had happened but she thought I was crazy.

The next week I bought a dozen eggs each day, but I found no odd eggs at all. Meanwhile, my brother and I rode Sugar, my flying horse, to school.

The next week I bought more eggs. When I got home, I opened the carton and there was one orange egg in the carton. I took the egg and cracked it. Out came a little tree. I took the tree and planted it in our front yard.

The next morning I woke up and looked out my window at my little tree. I couldn't believe my eyes! It was a real money tree. I took all the money I could reach. I took it into the house and counted it. I had one-hundred and fifty-three dollars and this was only the first day!

The next day I bought another dozen eggs. This time the odd egg was red. I cracked it open and there stood a little machine. On the machine was a tag which read "Homework Machine."

That week I rode my horse to school every day. I picked a thousand dollars from my tree every day, and I had an 'A' on every paper every day.

But the next Monday when I woke up, everything was gone, the horse, the money tree, and the homework machine. I asked my mother about these things. She laughed and said I had been dreaming. Only I know the truth!

Liz

Bird Brain

Once upon a time there was a beautiful young girl who lived in Japan. Her name was Sue Ling. She was an 'A' student in the tenth grade. She was also a very popular girl but she had one problem. Her parents and sister were nightingales. She had always longed to be like them but whenever she tried to sing the sound came out all wrong. When she tried to fly, she broke her nose.

One day when she came home from school, she found a note which read: "Dear Sue Ling, we have flown to America to go shopping. Should be back by six o'clock. Love, Ma, Pa, and Sis."

She waited all day for them to return but they never appeared. On the news she heard that there had been a thunderstorm, a hurricane, and tornado, all at one time, that had hit on her parents' route to the U.S. She thought of some terrible things that might have happened. Then she thought, "I must find them, but how?"

Sue Ling concentrated on being a nightingale even more. She thought of her parents and her sister and of how much she loved each one. She fell down and when she stood up, she had become a beautiful eagle.

"What? An eagle!" she said loudly.

Then she heard a loud voice say, "How are you supposed to fly through that terrible weather to save your family if you're just a little ol' nightingale?"

She was so excited she leaped into the air and away she flew.

Many days passed as she covered the entire ocean except for one uncharted deserted island. There she landed and found her family—dead.

Then she thought to herself, "It's all my fault. If I would have told them how much I loved them they would not be dead."

POP! POP!! She changed back to being a girl. "Oh, dear, how will I ever get off this island," she thought. "I'll die, too."

Just then she noticed a beautiful bottle on the shore. She picked it up and—PUFF-SWISH!—out came a genie. She fell down with delight.

"Master, your wish is my command," said the genie.

"Oh, hello," said Sue Ling.

"Hello," said the genie. "Please make a wish."

"Hmmm, what shall I wish—I know," said Sue. "I wish my family was alive."

Within an instant, there was her family, alive and asking questions.

After Sue Ling answered all the questions, she made another wish. "I wish I was an eagle again." She became an eagle. She made two more wishes. She wished for a flying carpet and she wished that the genie would always be hers.

The flying carpet appeared. The genie said to Sue Ling, "I will always be your genie."

They all climbed onto the carpet and took a trip around the

45

world before going home.

And by the way, since Sue Ling was an eagle, she became the national bird of the United States.

Zander McCall

The Calico Cow

There was once a brown cow in the land of Moo. She had just given birth to a calf. Much to her surprise, the calf was calico.

One year went by and Caliconia, called Calico by her friends, was now tipping the scales at two thousand pounds.

Just think how awful her mother felt every time she bought clothes for her. "Well," said her mother, "there has to be a stop to this."

Later that week, Calico and her mother visited a health spa. There they talked with the manager, Clerra Cow.

"What can we do about Calico?" asked her mother.

"Well, let's get started by having Bob and Bill Bull show her around a bit," answered Clerra Cow.

"I know them," said Calico. "They're in my class at school."

"Well, then, let's go," replied Clerra.

"Hi," said the twins at the same time.

"These two boys will show you around and if you want to stop and try any of the machines, just say so," said Clerra.

"Up and down, up and down, so many stairs in this place! How do you go so fast?" groaned Calico.

"These are nothing. We walk them every day," said Bob.

"Yeh, that's how we keep so slim and trim," bragged Bill.

As the days went on, pounds came off Calico. The day finally came for Calico's last physical at the spa.

"Come in and sit down, Calico. I have some good news for you," the doctor said. "You have taken off over five-hundred pounds and have reached your goal. I'm happier than a Jersey cow at a milking contest!"

"Oh, thank you," answered Calico. "You won't be seeing me here again. I have these ugly pounds off and I'm keeping them off forever."

Tabatha Welles

The Great Space Chase

Once in a different galaxy far far away, a spaceship by the name of the *Merriam Webster*, was ready for battle. A bunch of special flying dogs kept attacking them. They bit the ship and made dents in it. The dogs were at war with the Flying Tom Cats. This had been going on for two years and the cats were winning. So the *Merriam Webster*, commanded by David Fast, went steaming to the Planet of the Dogs to see what the dogs were up to.

They went to the Planet of the Tom Cats first to get escorts to go to the Planet of the Dogs. David Fast knew the dogs were waiting for them so he told his crew to go to their battle stations and get ready for the attacking dogs. When the dogs saw the Tom Cats, they attacked. David fired his 357 magnum at the dogs which scared the dogs half to death. They ran away, screaming and running as fast as they could. They ran so far away they were never heard of nor seen again. The *Merriam Webster* then zoomed away.

Linda Indiana

Strawberries

There is a girl named Strawberry Patty. She is three feet tall, very skinny, and has long blonde hair.

One day Strawberry Patty was walking down the road. She saw a strawberry patch so she decided to pick just one strawberry. When she was eating it, it began to pour down rain. She ran all the way home. When she got there, she put on dry clothes and went to bed.

Next morning when she woke up, everywhere she looked, there were strawberries—on her bed, on the chairs, everywhere. She ran outside and everywhere she looked there were strawberries. Patty then went to the neighbors—strawberries everywhere!

She went back home and sat down in a chair. She thought about what had happened. While she was sitting there, thinking, she became hungry so she started eating the strawberries off the chair. She ate and ate and ate. Finally, she was full. She got a bad stomach ache and went to the doctor. The doctor said, "You have eaten so many strawberries that I am going to have to put you on a strawberry diet!" She fainted.

47

She went home and weighed herself. She weighed eight-hundred pounds because of all the strawberries she had eaten.

Patty decided to make some pies, cakes, and other things with the strawberries. She went to the strawberry patch and picked two-hundred baskets of strawberries. She made two-hundred strawberry pies, one-hundred strawberry cakes, ten boxes of strawberry candy, fifty dozen strawberry rolls, eighty jars of strawberry jam, and canned one-hundred jars of plain strawberries. She still has one-hundred acres of strawberries and they are still growing.

Strawberries now cover the whole state of North Dakota and half of the state of South Dakota.

Shirley Katz

Mountain Jack

One day Mountain Jack was in the woods cutting down trees. He is a three-foot giant with curly hair. He has muscles like a U.S. tank.

All of a sudden, the ground started to shake and there was a great explosion. Out came lava from a volcano.

He ran down to the town of Sham Rock, which was nearby, and told everyone to ride to the next town to be out of danger. Everyone left.

Mountain Jack ran back up the mountain and said to himself, "I'll have to find some huge boulders."

He kept looking around for some. There, behind a tree, was a huge boulder. With his mighty strength he picked up the boulder and threw it up to the top of the volcano and it rolled into the hole. It stopped the lava from coming out.

He ran down the mountain, went into his house, and went to bed. The next day he went to the next town to get all of the people and brought them back to their homes. They came back and had a big celebration. They made Mountain Jack the town's forest ranger.

Tyrone Jones